Alternatives to Running Away

This book is **dedicated to all the teenagers** *who won't make it home safe tonight.*

Erica's Choices is a program of
MISSING CHILDREN MINNESOTA
P.O. BOX 11216
MINNEAPOLIS, MN 55411

Dedicated to the safe return of all missing children.

Missing Children Minnesota Publications
Copyright 1996

Missing Children Minnesota
P.O. Box 11216 • Minneapolis, MN 55411
612•521•1188

All rights reserved. No part of this book may be reproduced or transmitted in any form or by any means, electronic or mechanical, including photocopying, recording, or copying by any information storage and retrieval system without prior written permission of Missing Children Minnesota.

ISBN 0-9641123-3-7

Printed in the United States Of America

The headlines on the cover are reprinted with permission of the Minneapolis Star Tribune Newspaper.

table of contents

- **4** • Thanks
- **5** • Introduction: Note To Young People
- **6** • Note to Parents
- **7** • Note to Teachers
- **8** • To The Three Men Who Killed Erica by Brandy Haneca
- **9** • Original Poster
- **10** • Erica's Story
- **12** • Erica Will Never . . .
- **14** • Erica, In Her Own Words
- **20** • Erica's Friends & Family
- **28** • You Have Choices
- **30** • If You Are On The Run
- **32** • If A Friend Is On The Run
- **34** • Self-Protection Strategies
- **36** • Making Good Choices
- **37** • Map of Erica's Choices
- **38** • Map of Your Choices
- **39** • Statistics On Runaways
- **40** • Questions You Can Ask Yourself
- **52** • Your Journal

thanks

Thanks first of all to Erica's mother and stepfather, Linda and Lennis Stavne, for permission to use Erica's story, her writings and photos, and those of her brother and sisters to help other kids. Thank you to Brenda Lantz, Brandy Haneca and her parents, and Harmony Sauke and her parents for their permission to include what they wrote about Erica. Special thanks to the Minneapolis Star Tribune Newspaper for permission to reprint the headlines on the cover of the book.

I also want to thank everyone at Missing Children Minnesota who made this book possible: Sylvia Alzouhayli, LaJeanne Runnels, Angela Ariss, and the Board of Directors. Special thanks to Jackie Beach at Graffic Traffic, for all her help with desktop publishing, design, editing, proofing and putting up with me; and to Glenna Lewis for constant encouragement, friendship and publishing expertise. Thanks to my parents, George and Elizabeth Watson, for helping me get through my own teenage years relatively unscathed, and to my husband, Richard Olson, and our sons, Leif and Eric, who share me with the world when they would really rather have my time all to themselves.

introduction to young people

This book is for you. It begins with Erica's story. It's a true story. Erica was a real person who lived, and died at the age of 14. She died because of a few bad choices she made. I hope this book will help you think about the choices you make. We all make bad choices; Erica didn't deserve to die for her mistakes, but she did anyway.

This book is based on a program I developed for junior and senior high school-aged young people after Erica was murdered. I began telling her story in hopes it would help other kids stop and think about the consequences of their actions before going on the run. It has evolved into this book about making better choices and staying safe.

This book is also a journal for you to use to write about your feelings and work out your problems. You may have kept a journal before for a school assignment, but this is **just for you.** No one is going to collect this and read it or put a grade on it; it's private. I created this book for you because I believe if young people understand the **dangers** of running away from home and the **alternatives,** they will make the choice to be safe.

This book also includes a section about personal safety because half the children kidnapped by someone outside their family (a stranger or acquaintance) are age twelve or older. Don't make the mistake of thinking that you couldn't be a victim -- it can happen to anyone. It just makes sense to do some simple things to keep safe.

This is the second edition of **Erica's Choices.** You can help make the next edition better by sharing your thoughts about this second edition with me. If you have something to share or a suggestion about this book, please write to me: Carol Watson, Missing Children Minnesota, P.O. Box 11216, Minneapolis, MN 55411. Remember, you have a lot of good things ahead of you to stay safe for!

to parents

As a mother, I can tell you that one of the most devastating things a parent can experience is not knowing where your child is and if he or she is safe. I know, because my oldest son was missing for 13 months when he was just a toddler, and I can tell you, not knowing is the hardest part. Most of us have experienced panic for brief periods when a child wandered off in a department store or came home later than expected. This is just a small taste of what it is like to have a child missing. As executive director of Missing Children Minnesota, I have worked since 1983 assisting families of missing children in their search and I can tell you that it doesn't matter how old your child is or even if your child left of his or her own free will in anger -- a parent's anguish over a missing child cannot be measured.

This book, and the Erica's Choices program it's based on, came about as a response to the pointless and tragic death of Erica Grothe and the dramatic rise in the number of runaway cases that I have witnessed in recent years. I have seen too many "Erics and Ericas" who didn't make it home and many more who came home, tragically hurt, emotionally and physically, by their experiences on the street. This book is written in the firm belief that if young people are given the real facts about running away from home, and some viable, safe alternatives, there will be fewer kids making unsafe choices.

You will find some statistics on page 39 which show that children run away from home for many reasons. The majority of teens on the run say they left home because of "family problems." Communication between parents and teens seems to be a critical factor. It is always important that we listen to our children and take their concerns seriously. It is also important that we respect their privacy. The journaling pages of this book should be private unless your son or daughter decides to share them with you. The questions in the book can be used as a starting point for discussions, but be sure that you are respectful of their ideas and their need for space.

The statistics also tell us that 16% of kids on the run say they left home because of physical, emotional, or sexual abuse. If your child is experiencing any kind of abuse at home, his/her risk of running away is greatly increased. **No one deserves to live in an abusive home.** Please take steps **NOW** to end the abuse and start the healing process.

The Child Abuse Hotline can help you find resources in your area. Talk to your minister, call the school counselor, call the police, call someone; **get help -- do it now -- for both you and your child! Child Abuse Hotline: 1-800-4-A CHILD.**

I hope you never have to deal with a missing child, but if it should happen, there are resources available. The National Center for Missing and Exploited Children can help and they can also refer you to resources in your area. **To Report a Missing Child, Call: 1-800-843-5678 (1-800-THE-LOST).**

Finally, if you have experiences, information or comments to share please write me: Carol Watson, Missing Children Minnesota, P.O. Box 11216, Minneapolis, MN 55411.

to teachers

The Erica's Choices program this book is based on has been used in classrooms and with groups of youth for several years. This book can be used as a blueprint for a classroom unit on making better choices, but I urge you to respect your student's journaling in this book as private. The journal pages should not be used as homework assignments to be collected and graded. This is space for them to work out their own problems and feelings without fear of judgment by anyone. If some of your students choose to share them with you, you should feel privileged that they trust you so much.

Please note in the statistics on page 39 that 13% of teens on the run cite school or peer pressure as their reason for running. As a teacher, you may be the one person who can see and respond to a child in crisis. You may be the one person who can guide a child to the resources available and make the difference between that child getting help or making a bad choice with tragic consequences. Teachers are often the unsung heroes of our children's lives. Thank you for all that you do!

If you have experiences or insights to share for future editions of **Erica's Choices,** please write to me: Carol Watson, Missing Children Minnesota, P.O. Box 11216, Minneapolis, MN 55411.

to the three men who killed Erica*

Erica was my best friend. The kind of friend that anyone would love to have. You could tell her anything and she would listen. If you had a problem she would be there to help you, and before you knew it, it wasn't a problem anymore. If I was sad, she would always make me laugh. Her smile could brighten any sad face.

Now I don't have anyone to make me laugh, because one cold December night, three young men decided to take that away forever. I wonder how they would feel if their best friend was murdered? I have many mixed feelings. Especially anger and hate, because they thought they could play God and end a life that wasn't theirs to end.

I guess no matter what the law gives these 3 people, in my eyes and heart it will never be enough. Not even if it's life plus a day. But someday God will be the judge, and justice will be done.

Brandy Haneca

BRANDY AT AGE 14

✘ Read at the trial of each of the three men who killed Erica

ORIGINAL POSTER

PLEASE POST

SINCE: 10-26-92
CASE # 2-797

MISSING

FROM: Granite Falls, MN
POSTER ISSUED: 11-23-92

ERICA LYNN GROTHE

*Erica,
Could you please call and
let us know that you are
alright – PLEASE!
We Love You*

Born: 8/15/78 **Build:** Medium **Hair:** Dark Brown **Eyes:** Brown
Height: 5'1" **Weight:** 105 lbs. **Age:** 14

PLEASE CALL:
**National Center for
Missing & Exploited Children**
800-THE LOST
OR NATIONAL RUNAWAY SWITCHBOARD
800-621-4000
Copyright ©1992 Missing Children Minnesota
Box 11216 • Minneapolis, Minnesota 55441

(612) 521-1188

MISSING CHILDREN MINNESOTA
Dedicated to the safe return of all missing children.

This poster was made possible by
donations from concerned citizens.

Erica's story

Erica was a fourteen-year-old girl from a small town in Minnesota. She was a lot like the other girls in her town or any town. Her family had moved a lot. Her parents were divorced and her mother remarried and then separated from her stepfather, but eventually they got back together. Her mother said Erica's problem was she was a fourteen-year-old who wanted to be eighteen. She dated older boys and eventually got into trouble for stealing and ended up in a group home in another town 35 miles away. This particular group home was actually a farm with horses and Erica loved animals. She was happy there and doing well.

A few days before halloween a couple of other girls at the group home persuaded Erica to go on the run with them to Minneapolis. We don't know exactly why Erica went with them, but it seems to have been a spur-of-the-moment decision, probably due to peer pressure.

Erica's mother contacted Missing Children Minnesota for help in finding her. We made a poster of Erica and had it circulated throughout the city. The day after Thanksgiving, Erica called her mom to say she was okay and she would come home soon. She said, "I don't belong here. I'll be home for Christmas."

Erica didn't make it home for Christmas. On December 8, 1992, just a week after she had called her mother, Erica was murdered. Three men entered the apartment where she was babysitting. Two of them held her down while the third put a .357 caliber revolver with one bullet in it to her head and pulled the trigger twice and nothing happened. He then loaded a second bullet into the gun, put the gun to her head and pulled the trigger again, killing her instantly. The reason they gave for killing her was that she had lied about her age. They said she had sex with the man who pulled the trigger and when he found out she was fourteen and not seventeen he was afraid he would get into trouble for sleeping with an under-age girl. They later denied that was the reason for killing her, but they never gave another explanation.

Erica's murder received wide coverage in the news the next few days and because Missing Children Minnesota had circulated posters on Erica, several TV reporters came to our office to interview me (Carol Watson) about Erica. One asked me, "What does it mean that Erica is dead?" I thought for a moment and replied, "Erica will never get to grow up. She will never open her Christmas presents or go to the prom. She will never learn how to drive a car or have her own money to spend on whatever she wants. She will never graduate from high school, get married, have children. Her life is just over." It makes me sad even now to think that, because of a few bad choices, she will never get to hug her mother again.

Erica made some bad choices, but she didn't deserve to pay for them with her life. Everyone makes mistakes, but if you can realize that you have made a bad choice and turn around and make a better choice before it's too late, you don't have to end up like Erica. At least half a million kids run away from home each year. Most come back within a few days, but every year some, like Erica, don't ever make it home again. If you want to know about Erica, turn to pages 14-27 for things Erica and her friends and family have written.

Erica will never...

get to open her **Christmas Presents**

go on **Vacation**

learn how to **Ski**

go to the **Prom**

Graduate from high school

have another **Boyfriend**

have a **Job** and have her own **Money**

get **Married**

become a **Mom**

get a **driver's License**

have her own **Car**

hug her **Mom**

what do you have to look *forward* to?

Erica, in her own words

ERICA, AGE 5

Erica Grothe's Bio 8/18/92

My name is Erica Lynn Grothe. I was born August 15, 1978, at 7:32 a.m. at the St. Joseph Hospital in Mankato, MN. I weighed 6 lbs. and 2 oz.

I have an older sister whose name is Anna and she is 16. I have a younger sister who is 13 and her name is Amy. I also have a younger brother whose name is Chad. Last of all, I have another sister who is seven and her name is Ashley. My mom's name is Linda Stavne, my-step dad's name is Lennis Stavne, and my real dad's name is Tom Grothe.

I don't really remember much about my early childhood. I do know that my mom has always had custody of me and I don't remember hardly anything about her. I remember only certain parts of my childhood. Like about the day my mom and step-dad got married. My mom asked what I was going to call Lennis. From that day on I remember things about her. I wish I knew why I don't remember some things about her. I don't really think she was around a lot. We've lived in many different towns and we've had to change schools quite often along with it.

I was born in Mankato but I didn't go to school there until the eighth grade. The first school I went to was in Granite Falls. I also went to school in St. Cloud, Holdingford, Avon, Albany, Kimball, Sauk Rapids, Becker, and Canby. The longest I ever stayed in a school was for 2 years.

It wasn't hard on me at first to move around so often, but after I got into junior high it caught up with me. I've always made friends easily and received good grades so at least I had somewhat of an advantage.

I started to get into trouble when I moved to Sauk Rapids with my mom after her and my step-dad split up. Pretty soon I had a 16-year-old boyfriend and was always getting into trouble with my friends. Then I had to go to court for theft because I was with a friend when she stole something. Before I knew it I had to go to court for truancy and going on the run.

Eventually I got sent away to a group home in Becker for violating my probation. It was hard being away from home at first because it was a totally new set-up for me.

Before I went to the group home, as I said before, my boyfriend was 16. I was only 12. I really cared about him and he said that he really loved me, but it didn't last because I got sent away to Becker and he fell in love with my best friend. It was hard at first but I had to face it. From then on I've always had older boyfriends and have acted older than my age.

After I left the group home I went and lived with my paternal grandmother in Madison Lake. It didn't work out there because she was way too strict, even my P.O. [probation officer] said that she was. I ended up running from there a couple of times because she wouldn't even hardly let me go outside, except to take her dog out or unless I was with her.

ERICA, AGE 5

When I couldn't stay there anymore, I went back to the group home. From the day I got to the group home the second time, it was decided that I was to go to the Kandiyohi Girls Group Home in Willmar. But instead, on the day of court, my mom got an attorney and they decided that I would get to go home, only for three weeks though, just to try it out. If I got along good at home then I could stay. But it didn't work out, because I only thought it would work, I didn't even try to make it work.

Then I ended up going to a foster home in Canby. I also ended up running from there because I hated my foster parents. They were always putting my family down and making me feel really bad about who I was.

Only if I would've listened to my mom when she told me to watch out for what I was doing. Today I'm trying to sort out my problems and get through each day looking forward to the next. This way I won't want to run because here, I know that someone will be here to help me through each day, so I won't have to do it on my own.

Myself

what i like...

shape of eyes
my honesty
skin color
hair
voice
how I get along with people
how I can cook certain things
school grades
easy to get along with
friendships
relationship with parents
health

what i don't like...

eye color
teeth
fingernails
argumentative
attitude towards authority
no patience
frustration
scars on face
my apparent male issue
relationship with Anna
previous history

(this piece is untitled and not dated)

 I swear to god, these people want me to go on the run! Unfortunately I'm not about to give them the pleasure! I'm going through a lot of crap now and I assume some people want to add to my troubles. If I run from here it would be pointless! (and stupid!) I have so much going for me and this is my last chance to get my life together and my problems sorted out. No - I'm gonna take this opportunity and make it very worthwhile. I'm proud of myself because I've managed to face a lot here and I haven't run yet - AND DON'T PLAN TO!!! - no matter what!!!

Erica's poetry

ALONE
Nobody Cares,
Nobody wants to listen,
Nobody feels what I go through
Nobody understands.

I am human
I deserve better,
Somebody should care,
And if someone does
I haven't met him or her yet.

Maybe it was meant this way,
Maybe it's me that has to care,
Maybe "I" have to listen to myself
Obviously no one else is going to.

"I" have to live through it all,
"I" have to help myself,
Help Myself to see the rainbows,
The rainbows at the end of every storm.

My whole life has been a storm,
So maybe soon I will understand,
Understand that I can force that rainbow.

Erica's Letter to her mother

Dear Mom,

I know that I see you every weekend but I decided to write to you because I know that I like to get letters in the mail, even if they don't really say anything.

I just wanted to tell you and dad how much you and your support mean to me. I mean if you guys weren't supportive of me I wouldn't try to get anywhere in the program. I don't know if you guys realize how much I depend on you for your love and support.

I'm so looking forward to moving home again. At first I wasn't sure if I wanted to because I didn't know what it would be like, but now, I see what it's like and I 'm really excited! I've noticed a major change in the way you've taken control and the kids listen to you. I've also noticed how well you've been getting along and agreed on a lot of decisions.

I just wanted to send you a letter telling you how much you mean to me and how important you are.

Don't ever forget how important you are to us kids and don't ever doubt us or give up on any of us, because we depend on you to give us encouragement.

Lots Of Love.
Your daughter,
Erica L. Grothe

CHAD, AMY, ERICA, ANNA

erica's friends & family

ANNA, 11 • ERICA, 9 • AMY, 8
CHAD, 5 • ASHLEY, 3

a note from Erica's parents

When Carol [Carol Watson of Missing Children Minnesota] first asked us to write about Erica we were not sure we could. All we could think to say was, "We had a beautiful daughter named Erica and now she's gone." But there is a lot more to say about Erica. She was not only beautiful, but smart and funny and loving and frustrating and kind and willful and challenging all at the same time. She loved animals and people and her favorite color was purple. She loved to be the center of attention, which can be a problem when, like Erica, you have three sisters and a brother. She wanted to be a writer or maybe a veterinarian. She was a good student, she would have graduated from high school this year. She could have been anything she wanted, and now she will never have that chance.

We know we made mistakes. We weren't perfect parents. No one ever is. Erica didn't have an easy life. Maybe we should have been stricter or something, but we did the best we could. When she ran away from the group home we tried very hard to find her. With the help of Missing Children Minnesota we distributed hundreds of posters.

Her murder has left a huge hole in our hearts; a pain that will never go away. It has been so hard. We haven't really had a chance to grieve for her; every time we start to try to deal with it something else happens, and it is frightening to think of experiencing the pain we have kept bottled up. It feels as if it will overwhelm us and drown us in sorrow. The holidays and birthdays are especially hard. We keep going because we know that Erica would want us to take care of the other children.

This tragedy didn't end when Erica was killed; her brother and sisters have all had problems since she died. All of us who loved her carry it with us every day. After the wake and the funeral and putting her into the ground we had to try to help her brother and sisters and her close friends deal with their pain, too. We sat through three trials and each of the men involved in her murder was convicted. It was so hard to hear the testimony and see the crime scene pictures, but we had to do it for Erica - we had to see it through to the end.

The man who pulled the trigger and killed our daughter read a statement in court after he was convicted. He said he had gotten to know her in the weeks before her murder and that he knew Erica would forgive him for what he had done. You know, he's right -- Erica was like that; she would have forgiven him -- but it's not that easy for us. We will spend the rest of our lives trying to deal with what happened to our beautiful daughter, but we hope that her story will help other young people make the choice to be safer. Erica would have liked that; she loved helping people; she loved to be the center of attention; and in a way, her dream of being a writer has come true.

Linda and Lennis Stavne
Granite Falls, Minnesota, March, 1996

to the men who killed my sister*

Wanted to write to you because I cannot talk to you.
Want you to know how mad I am at you because you killed my sister. I am very sad, too, because you took my sister away. I love my sister Erica very much and will miss her.
　　　NO MORE KILLING ANYONE ANYMORE!
　　　NO MORE SHOOTING GUNS!
　　　NO MORE HEAD LOCKS!
I will not be able to kiss her or hug her or let her know that I love her very much because you killed her. You should pay for this crime forever. I shut my eyes and cry hoping when I open my eyes Erica Lynn will be hugging me. I love her a lot.

　　　　　　　　　　　　　　From Chad Stavne - Erica's brother
　　　　　　　　　　　　　　Written at age 10

Erica*

I love my sister Erica very much. She is a very special sister to have and very pretty. I can't give her a kiss or a hug anymore because three men killed her. They are very stupid to have killed her. My sister is the one that taught me how to do a lot of stuff. I was sad when she was killed. I think about her all the time. I cry for her all the time. She means a lot to me. My sister is the one who used to go out to the ranch. She would show me the animals out on the ranch. My sister is very smart. When she was killed she was fourteen years old. She was born August fifteenth, 1978, in Mankato, Minnesota. She was baptized at St. Peter's Lutheran church. Erica loved horses. She has a ribbon for Horse Shows. She was very good with animals. I love her hugs and kisses, and now I don't get them from her because she is dead.

　　　　　　　　　　　　　　Love,
　　　　　　　　　　　　　　Ashley Marie - Erica's sister
　　　　　　　　　　　　　　Written at age 9

✻ Read at the trial, November 30, 1993

excerpt from a statement by Erica's aunt, Brenda Lantz*

To whom this may concern:

...Erica's family should not be picking out what color Erica's memorial stone should be, they should be wondering what color her prom dress is going to be! But Erica will never have the chance to go to the prom, graduate from high school, go to college, get married or have children of her own — all because three people decided to take matters into their own hands and played God for a day! You took all her dreams away from her, and you took her away from us.

Now you people think that your charges and bail should be lowered. Why do you think you should have any rights at all? Where were Erica's rights when she was at the mercy of your hands?

The second reason I am writing is because of my own children and how Erica's death has affected them. I have a four-year-old daughter who is afraid to go to sleep at night because she dreams about the bad people who killed her cousin and she is afraid that they will get out of jail and come and kill her next. Ever since Erica died, she is obsessed with death, she thinks that all of her friends are going to die. I don't think that is normal for a four-year-old child.

My other daughter is always asking, "Why did God make bad people?" How do you explain that God didn't make people bad, the people make themselves bad!

You have taken away a lot more from us than Erica!!! You have also taken away our feelings of security and safety, and yes, even some our faith in people! I guess being born in a small town I have always been a bit naive. I have always trusted people, and believed that all people had good in them, but since the murder of my niece I don't believe that anymore...

 Read at the trial of each of the three men who killed Erica

Erica's best friend
Erica Lynn Grothe - tuesday, 8/29/95
by Brandy Haneca

My name is Brandy Haneca, Erica was my best friend she meant a lot to me. We did a lot of stuff together. I'll never forget Erica or the fun times we had together.

The first moment I met Erica I liked her. We were in Clarkfield at the school eating lunch and someone introduced me to her. I liked her from the start. I asked her if I could stay at her house that weekend and her mom said yes. From that moment on we were together always. We shared lockers cuz we always wanted to be with each other. That weekend I stayed at Erica's and met her mom, Linda. I really took to Linda because there was something special about Linda always telling Erica she loved her and always hugging her. Erica and Linda were close and it was a special kind of closeness. Erica could tell Linda anything and she'd understand. To this day I see Linda as my second mom. Erica really loved her mom and was always talking about her.

Erica and I used to sneak out of the house together. We would sometimes baby-sit together and the kids just adored Erica. We sure had a lot of fun times together. Erica was the light of my life, I looked up to Erica because of her relationship with her mom, and because she was always laughing, happy, smiling. She was a beautiful young girl and guys were always attracted to her.

When Erica got sent away I always tried to know where she was. All I knew is that she was in Canby then sent to some girls' home. Then I heard she ran away.

I knew something awful would happen to Erica. When I found out Erica got killed I didn't believe it at first cuz I didn't find out in a very nice way. I was on the bus to Clarkfield with all my classmates and someone stood up and goes, " Yeah Brandy, last night Erica got shot." And they started laughing. That is not a thing you joke about. When I got to school, I asked Erica's sister Amy, and she said it was true. I went running to my school counselor crying and she comforted me. When I got home I walked up to the door and my mom asked me what was wrong and I told her, so she called Linda. Linda asked me to be a pallbearer and I said I would, that really meant a lot to me. People didn't think I could be a pallbearer but I had to do it for Erica and for myself. At Erica's wake she didn't really look like the beautiful young girl I once knew. What really got me mad was that the kids on the bus who were so rude when told me about Erica were only there to see what Erica looked like. They could have at least had enough respect to tell me about her death in a decent way.

After Erica's death I wasn't able deal with it - it's been really hard for me. I started getting into alcohol, then pot and then I started doing crank and every kind of over-the-counter drug I could get my hands on to deal with the pain from Erica's death. I went to treatment for the drugs and am clean now and have learned to deal with Erica's death. Right after Erica died, I would have dreams about her. I had a dream that I was back at Erica's funeral and everything took place in order. I've had dreams of Erica coming back to life and telling me how she got killed. I've seen all the guys that killed Erica and they're not the kind of guys she would normally hang around with, but she was desperate after she ran away, though, and had no other place to go. She thought it was fun until she really got to know them.

The guys who killed her should have gotten a lot more time than they did because if you kill someone you kill them - there's no other way to look at it. I have a lot of mixed feelings for the guys who did it - anger, hate, and confusion. Erica was just a young innocent girl that had a whole life ahead of her. Erica had dreams and goals that she wanted to accomplish, but three men decided to take that away from her forever. Erica never tried to hurt anyone and I just wish I knew what really went on that lead to Erica's death.

BRANDY 1996

How do I begin to say goodbye to my best friend? The pain back once again. It's the worst pain in the world, that all friends have to experience. BUT, God put us on earth for a special reason and God takes us back home for a special reason and only when this happens to us will we know the answer.

Erica, I know you're with God now and you will be well taken care of, but it's hard for me to understand that, because I'm going to miss your smile, our little talks and how you always cheered me up when I was sad. I'll always remember those special memories and I'll laugh and cry, but I'll remember and treasure them.

Well Erica, I guess this is it, I hate to say it, but I know I have to, Goodbye, best friend, until we meet again someday.

Best Friends,
Brandy Haneca

if you had a friend who was *murdered like Erica* how would you feel

I would feel very hurt and depressed & I would really hate the people who killed her. I would probabely want to punish the people who killed her so they could no what its like not to have a friend around that you can talk to because they would be in prison & wouldn't have any contact.

poem by an anonymous friend of Erica's family

THE PAIN INSIDE

Although much time has past
   since the day that she died...
It seems just like yesterday
   because of the pain inside.

Although many have been there
   it's hard to confide..
Words just can't do justice
   because of the pain inside.

Although "lives must go on"
   oh, how hard we have tried...
We cannot move forward
   because of the pain inside.

Although we're here for each other
   and together we've cried...
Our issues are separate
   because of the pain inside.

Although before we had problems
   this we've never denied...
It's hard to deal with daily things
   because of the pain inside.

Although we live in one house
   we continue to hide...
Our feelings about her death
   because of the pain inside.

Although our family is strong
   with love, courage and pride...
together we'll hold on
   until this pain subsides.

you have choices

Every day of *your* life you make steps
that will take you on the journey
to the rest of your life.

You have the choice **now**
to begin taking steps toward the place
you want to be.

If you are thinking about *running* away, **DON'T**:
INSTEAD --

CALL a *friend*.
TALK to your *school counselor*.
CALL a *crisis hotline*.
GET *help*.
Make a list of *alternatives* and pick one!

my choices

- Think it over and decide the best option
- Call or talk to a good friend
-

if you are on the run...

STOP!!
GET OFF THE STREET NOW!!

GO to a *safe place*.
Do not go to a "crash pad" (an apartment or house that is open to kids on the street). That's where Erica ended up. They may say you can stay there for free, but eventually there will be a price to pay!

GO to a *shelter*.

GO to a *friend's home*.

CALL a *hotline* to find out where the nearest shelter is.

CALL your *parents*.
Let them know you are safe. They worry about you.

If you can't go home because of abuse, tell people why and *ask for help!*

my options

- would be to call someone and let them know I am OK
- Go home where I'd be a lot safer
- go to a friends
- go to a relatives

if you have a friend who is on the run

or is talking about running . . .

BE a *friend* and try to help.

HELP your *friend* find an alternative.

Call one of the crisis hotlines with your *friend*.

Talk to your *parents*.

Go with your *friend* to the school counselor or social worker.

DON'T

go on the run with your *friend*; you could both end up in a **dangerous situation!**

Even if you're not thinking about running:

TALK to your parents about any problems that come up.

HELP your school or community organize alternatives, like a peer counseling group, for kids who might consider running away.

KEEP little problems from developing into big ones.

FIND someone to talk with about what is bothering you.

my decisions

- tell her parents where she was going and who she was with. (if you knew)
- try to find her
- talk to her, help her

self-protection strategies

Don't make the mistake of thinking you can't be a victim because you're smart or strong or live in a small town or whatever. Everybody thinks "It will be okay this one time" or "I'm not that special" until something does happen. No one wants you to live a fearful life, but it just makes good sense to be careful. If safety precautions become a habit, you will be safer your whole life. Here are some tips for living safe.

- **trust your feelings.** Avoid dangerous situations and people. If something doesn't feel right to you, trust your instincts and get out of there -- now!

- **don't hitchhike.** It is one of the most dangerous things you can do.

- **use the "buddy system."** You are always safer when you are with other people.

- **make sure someone knows** where you're going, when to expect you home, and where to look for you if you don't show up when expected.

- **don't be too trusting** of people you don't know. If someone you don't know well suddenly wants to get close to you, ask yourself, "What does this person want from me?"

- **stay aware** of your surroundings and what resources are available to you. If you are walking with your head in the clouds or sitting at a bus stop with your nose in a book someone could surprise you!

- **if approached** by someone you don't trust, keep your distance. If you are close enough for someone to hand something to you, you are close enough for them to grab you.

- **if someone** does try to grab you or tries to hurt you physically or sexually, or tries to force you to go away with them:

    - **run** -- get away as fast as possible; go toward the closest safe place where there are people. Don't run to a lonely, deserted or secluded place!

    - **fight back**, only if you have to in order to get free. Don't stick around to get hurt. Remember the best fight is no fight – it's flight!

    - **yell** for help in a loud, deep voice; make as much noise as possible!

    - **tell** the authorities if you are attacked.

choices

Making ***good choices*** isn't something we are born knowing how to do. It's something we learn to do over time. Part of that learning process is making mistakes and realizing there is a better choice than the one we made. We all make hundreds of choices everyday -- what to wear, what to have for breakfast, who to sit with at lunch and so on.

Most of the choices we make are not life or death; chances are, no one will die if you wear a tee shirt instead of a flannel shirt. Other choices may not seem important at the time, like watching television instead of doing your home work. Some choices may have consequences that aren't obvious at first -- for instance, you may choose not to spend time with certain friends and then later realize you've lost their friendship because they felt you didn't care or didn't like them anymore.

Sometimes it is easier to think of choices in a visual way. You can draw a decision or choice map to help you understand how the choices you make branch out.

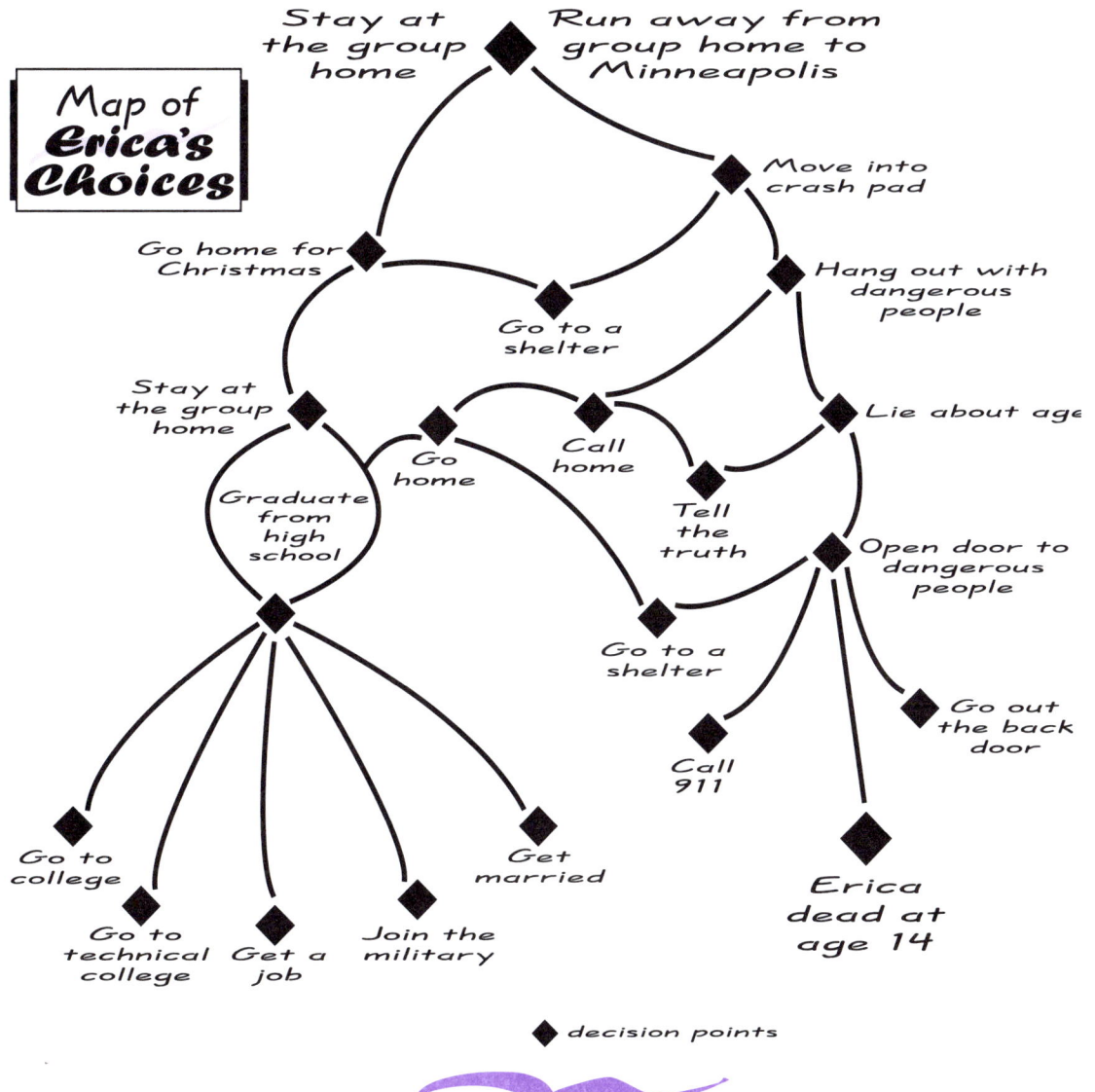

This map shows only **some of the choices Erica could have made.** As you can see, sometimes you can go backward and sometimes you can't. You might try making a choice map of your own -- what are your choices and where will they lead you? As you can see, Erica had lots of options all the way until the very end. Think about other choices Erica could have made. SOMETIMES YOU DON'T KNOW WHERE A CHOICE WILL LEAD YOU. Wouldn't it be better to try to always choose a safer option instead of one that could lead to dangerous situations?

Try spending a day thinking about all the choices you make, big and small. Try thinking about one specific choice and what it might mean a week from now or a month from now. **If you discover that you've made a choice you wish you could change, think about ways to do that.**

map of my choices

- become a pshychiatrist
- go to college
- graduate from high school
- get married
- have kids

stats

Each year approximately ***1 to 1.5 million children*** run away from home.
(National Runaway Switchboard, 1994)

Over 200,000 of them will become involved in ***high risk behavior,*** such as drug use or prostitution.
(Children's Defense Fund, 1986)

Each year ***3,600 to 4,200 children*** *are abducted* by someone outside the family; half of them are age 12 or older; 2/3 are female; at least 19% of these abductors are not strangers to their victims. ***2/3 of the victims of "stranger" abduction homicide are 14-17 years old.***
(Finklehor, p.10)

70% of runaways return home or are reunited with their families. ***The rest become victims of violence, crime, prostitution, child pornography, or starvation on the streets.***
(Rosenbaum, p. 261)

40% of runaways engage in some form of hustling or prostitution.
(Palenski p. 90)

72% of youth use drugs while engaged in prostitution.
(Weisberg, p. 58)

48% of runaways are home within *3 days.*
21% are on the run for *4-7 days.*
14% are on the run for *1-4 weeks.*
9% are on the run for *1-2 months.*
5% are on the run for *2-6 months.*
3% are on the run for *more than 6 months.*

REASONS GIVEN FOR GOING ON THE RUN:
52% - *Family problems*
13% - *School or peer pressure*
8% - *Physical abuse*
4% - *Emotional abuse*
4% - *Sexual abuse*
Other reasons include pregnancy, alcohol or drug abuse, and legal issues.
(Children's Defense Fund, 1986)

questions

Read and think about the following questions. You have your own journal space throughout this book to write about your personal thoughts and feelings. **Take as much time as you want -- this is just for you!** Try to talk about some of these questions with your parents, or a teacher, a school counselor or a friend -- someone you know who cares. Also, there are some numbers you can call at the back of this book, including free "800" crisis phone lines. You can always call or write to me, Carol Watson, at Missing Children Minnesota, P.O. Box 11216, Minneapolis, Minnesota 55411.

what choices did Erica have when she was at the group home?

To go on the run with her friends to Minneapolis & be in danger or to stay there and get help and to have a chance to get to go home after her time was up.

why do you think Erica chose to run from the group home that night?

- Peer pressure
- She was sick of being in placement
- She was bored, needed something to do
- Felt that if she didn't she'd miss out on something

have you ever run away or thought about running away?

yes - I've ran away before a couple of times - the first few times that I ran I went to Marshall with my friends I was pretty safe except once & I got raped which scared me enough to realize that running was stupid. I also ran away with the carnival & decided it was dirty & really gross & the cops found me & brought me to Woodland Centers for 72 hours

why did you run (or think about running)? what happened to you?

Already answered on previous page

what would you do differently now?

Think about it alot more than I did & I wouldn't have run because it just causes trouble for me and everyone else.

how do you think Erica's mother felt when she was told her daughter had been murdered?

upset, sad, mad at the people who killed her

if you could say something to Erica today what would it be?

Not to run because it just causes trouble & it's very dangerous. I'd also tell her that she has friends & family who care about her & don't want her to get hurt

where could you go if you ever felt unsafe at home?

- relatives
- friends
- crisis centers

make a list of people
you can talk to or go to for help.

It could be anyone you trust - a relative, a teacher, a school counselor, your best friend's mom. Write their names and phone numbers here.

NAME	PHONE #
Sherry Stangeland	(320) 669-8809
Kristel Walters	(320) 669-7691

what could you do if a friend told you he or she was going to go on the run?

Tell them what has happened to me when I ran & tell them its not safe

what do you fight about
with your parents?

when I should or shouldn't be able to go out during the week
my curfew
what I do or don't do
how much I help out around the house

what else could you do to make your point, or feel in control (or whatever)?

sit down & say what I think is the best way without being interrupted

my journal

Bibliography

Children's Defense Fund. Building Health Programs for Teenagers, Washington D.C. 1986

Finklehor, David; Hotaling, Gerald; Sedlak, Andrea. Missing, Abducted, Runaway and Thrownaway Children in America. Executive Summary, May, 1990. U.S. Department of Justice.

National Runaway Switchboard. Runaway Curriculum Guide. 1994 Chicago, IL

Palenski, Joseph. Kids Who Run Away LC 83-622948. 1984

Rosenbaum, Alvin. The Young People's Yellow Pages. 1983

Weisberg, D. Kelly. Children of the Night: A Study of Adolescent Prostitution. 1985

resources

Missing Children Minnesota
(612) 521-1188

Covenant House Nine Line
1-800-999-9999

Runaway Switchboard
1-800-621-4000

Crisis Connection
(612) 379-6363

Cross Streets
(612) 771-0076

Project Off Streets
(612) 338-3103